How to Hook Your Kids on

Books

*Create a Love
for Reading
That Will Last
a Lifetime*

Karen O'Connor

THOMAS NELSON PUBLISHERS
Nashville • Atlanta • London • Vancouver

Published in Nashville, Tennessee, by Thomas Nelson, Inc., Publishers, and distributed in Canada by Word Communications, Ltd., Richmond, British Columbia, and in the United Kingdom by Word (UK), Ltd., Milton Keynes, England.

Library of Congress Cataloging-in-Publication Data

O'Connor, Karen, 1938-
    How to hook your kids on books : create a love for reading that will last a lifetime / Karen O'Connor.
      p. cm.
    ISBN 0-7852-7942-3
    1. Children—United States—Books and reading.   I. Title.
Z1037.A103 1995
649'.58—dc20
                                        94-44159
                                          CIP

Printed in the United States of America
1 2 3 4 5 6 7 - 01 00 99 98 97 96 95

Dedicated to
my grandchildren
Noah, Johannah, Jacob, Liam, and Shevawn

and my step-grandchildren
Jordan, Matthew, Jacob, and Rachel

and their parents
with love!

Read! It's life itself!

—*Maurice Sendak*
children's author and artist

————————————

If you don't read you'll only be as big as your own life and your experiences. Books give you other centuries, other cultures, all kinds of people that you wouldn't otherwise know. Don't ever let life seem little or boring.

—*Jean Fritz*
children's author

Contents

Part 3:
Foster Reading Enrichment

Introduction

Bring children and good books together at an early age and you will create a friendship that will last a lifetime. Books strengthen, inspire, motivate, and encourage healthy self-esteem and foster understanding, affection, and respect for others. The child who reads opens a window on the world no one can close.

And what better place to receive the nurture of a good book than in one's home? In this familiar and comfortable setting, children can meet such endearing characters as Ramona and Beezus of the famed Beverly Cleary books; Ma, Pa, Laura, and Mary from the Little House stories; William and his doll from Charlotte Zolotow's beloved picture book; and humorous characters such as Carl the dog and Frances the badger.

Later they will grow to love authors of inspiring young adult books, such as Madeleine L'Engle, Kathryn Patterson, Richard Peck, and others, as they explore the world of growing up and making life-changing decisions.

Most book-loving families agree that if they foster literacy and the love of reading during their children's early years, the tradition soon becomes as integral to their routine as shared meals and family prayers.

It is not enough to wish or hope or talk about reading with your children. It is essential that we, as parents, *do* something about it. *How to Hook Your Kids on Books* provides that opportunity. There is something for everyone—ideas, activities, and projects that will help you bring books and your children together. This book is for anyone who wishes to encourage and foster reading in the children they love. You don't have to be knowledgeable in children's literature or recognize the names of children's book writers or be an accomplished reader yourself. And please don't feel discouraged if you can't implement all the ideas. This is a buffet. Choose what you like and leave the rest.

To start, all you need is a willing heart, this book, and at least one child. You can build from there. You may be a book lover yourself. And if not, in the process you may find that not only will the children in your life get hooked on books—but you will as well!

PART 1

Introduce Books

Read to Your Baby

In any bookstore today you will see books exclusively for babies. Most have nontoxic, chewable soft covers or are made of thick, sturdy cardboard with a shiny, wipe-and-clean surface. Some books are shaped like a bunny or puppy. Others are small and square—just right for little hands to hold. Still others look like a toy and make a good companion in the playpen, crib, or bathtub.

Baby books are booming! All this to show that it is never too early to introduce your children to books. Literacy does not start when a child reads his or her first words. It begins with reading readiness, a stage of development and growth where parents can take the lead.

Get Involved

Read to your baby, sing to your baby, play word games with your baby. According to Reading Is Fundamental, a national nonprofit organization that inspires reading in young people, "studies show that children who have books read to them at home learn to read more easily than those who don't."

It is never too early to introduce your little ones to books. Some mothers read to their children during pregnancy. Others open a book as soon as their child can focus on a page. Introduce your son or daughter to books in whatever way works for you.

Use books as creative tools for drawing out your baby's creativity, individuality, word play, and emotions.

Consistency is important. Take a few minutes each day to interact with your baby and a special book. Encourage sensory contact. Allow your baby to pat the book, touch it, hold it, even chew on it. These early books, with few exceptions, are meant to be used and loved—even worn out. This is not the time to teach reverence for the written word. Children can acquire that when they're a little older. At this point in your baby's life, it's probably best to spend your energy on simply making books available to your child.

Expand Your Baby's Experiences

Most books for the very young are simple picture books that focus on a single concept: interaction with family members, toys, animals, or the close-knit world of young children. This is a wonderful opportunity to use language in a colorful and creative way. You might even refer to real-life objects that match concepts you encounter in a book. For example, if you are going through an ABC book, show your child the picture then hold up a matching object such as an apple, ball, toy, or car.

If you have a dog or cat or bird in your home, choose books that show these animals, then point out the same creature in your baby's environment. None of these exercises is wasted. Even before your baby can speak, he is taking in sights and sounds and objects around him. As you share a book and corresponding points of reference in your baby's world, you will be helping him to build a relationship with books that will provide the foundation for a lifetime love of literature.

Mingle Books and Toys

Some parents separate books from toys in order to keep books safe and clean, away from eager little hands and mouths. I think it is wise to encourage children to respect books and to keep them in good condition so they can be enjoyed over and over and then passed on to siblings. But when children are very young—babies through toddler ages—we can make an exception to that rule. This is a time of exploration and discovery in a child's life. If we want our sons and daughters to grow up "hooked" on books, it is important to give them plenty of opportunities right from the start. Here are some suggestions to consider:

Set Up a Box for Books   Put a sturdy box within your child's reach and fill it with inexpensive baby and toddler books that children can touch and hold and play with. I've found such books in discount bookstores and in general stores, such as Everything's a Dollar. Look for nontoxic covers and childproof pages (usually plastic or durable cardboard). Include a few toys in the book box so children will begin to view books as something to enjoy as much as a favorite toy truck, doll, or ball.

Add Books to a Toy Box   If you already have a toy box, add a few books to the pile of toys—but be sure they are the inexpensive ones discussed above, because they're likely to get batted around a bit. But again, as long as your purpose is to expose books to your little ones, consider this an investment in their future.

Carry Books with You　A parent's diaper bag is generally well-stocked with bottles, diapers, wipes, a pacifier, teething ring, and a few favorite toys. Add a book or two. When your child is fussy, let her hold a book or, better yet, read the story to her or talk about the pictures as she holds (or chews on) the book.

Add Toddlers' Books to Family Bookshelf　Toddlers will take pride in having some of their books on the same shelf with books for other family members. Keep some favorite ones close at hand. If you're concerned about their being mishandled while children are still too young to understand good care, keep duplicates out of reach to be used only with supervision.

Expand the Listening Audience　Include dolls and stuffed animals. Encourage your preschoolers to "read" the story to these little friends. Use hand puppets to turn the pages or to take the part of one of the story's characters. Allow your children to invite a neighborhood friend or preschool classmate over for story time.

Buy Books with Your Children

Encourage your children's interest in books by letting them help in the selection process. One parent I know gives her children a sum of money to spend on books each month. This does not have to be a costly enterprise. Here are some ways to let your children participate in shopping for books:

Avenues for New Books

Bookstores Check your local bookstores for inexpensive new books, many available in paperback. Some stores offer discounts for quantity purchases or coupons to be redeemed for a free book after you buy a certain number. Put your name on the mailing list of local bookstores so you will be notified of special savings, promotions and clearances, author appearances, and book signing events.

Book Clubs Schools, parents' magazines, and some children's magazines offer opportunities for savings and good selection through book clubs that operate in a similar manner to adult book, music, and video clubs. Inquire at your local library, child's school, or at a neighborhood school if your children are of preschool age.

Toy Stores National chains usually have a children's book section with wide variety and substantial savings.

Mail Order Discount bookstores and remainder houses generally send catalogs to consumers a couple of times a year. Be on the lookout for such items. Good prices and a wide selection are available—with greater savings if you purchase a certain number.

Discount Stores Membership warehouses, such as Price Club/Costco, offer a good selection of children's books for a reasonable price. Stock changes frequently, so take your children along on your weekly or monthly shopping trip with the understanding ahead of time that they can purchase a book (not a toy).

School Book Fairs Schools offer discount rates on many fine children's paperback books and related materials such as bookmarks, posters, and cassette tapes. This is an easy way to provide your children with books and contribute to the school at the same time.

Gift Money Encourage your children to use a portion of cash gifts for books. Then take them shopping and let them make their own selections. I recommend that you plan ahead for this outing by discussing the kind of book they want to buy and the likely cost. Instead of making an impulsive purchase they may regret, they will be prepared to choose wisely. Sometimes they will still make a hasty choice and regret it later, but that's all right too. They will learn from these experiences as well.

The important thing is to give them the opportunity to be part of the selection process. This, in itself, is a great way to get to know the variety of books that are available on a wide range of topics. Your children are more likely to turn to books for education and entertainment when they see and find out for themselves what they have to offer.

Gift Books For gift-giving occasions, encourage relatives and friends to give your children books, magazine subscriptions, or membership in a book club in place of toys. Make your suggestions specific to the individual child. Learn each one's likes and interests. Offer a range of titles and prices so friends and family members can make an appropriate selection.

Avenues for Used Books

Family Storage   Look in attics, basements, garages, storage sheds—even hope chests—for old books. Perhaps you or a parent has saved some of your favorite books from childhood. If so, retrieve them and share them with your children.

Library Sales   Check with your local librarian for dates of used and donated book sales. Such fund-raising activities generally occur once or twice a year.

Trades   Your children can also acquire used books in good condition by trading with friends. You might even set up a book swap among neighborhood families.

Garage Sales, Flea Markets, Church Bazaars   Look through church bulletins, neighborhood newspapers, and organization newsletters for time and location of book sales.

Used Bookstores   Selections change frequently at such stores, so take your time visiting those in your area. You can locate many fine children's books at reasonable prices.

Resale and Thrift Shops   Goodwill and the Salvation Army, as well as many churches and veterans' groups, have stores with secondhand goods, including books. Selections change, so visit often to acquire the best titles.

Build a Home Library

If you're handy with wood and tools and so inclined, you and your children can build a bookcase from scratch or from a kit found at such stores as Home Depot, Homebase, and others. Children can participate in assembling it, setting it up, choosing a place for it, painting it, and stocking it. Add some comfortable seating and good lighting, and you'll have a fine mini-library.

Things to Consider

Location   Depending on available space, needs, and preferences, you might put one bookcase or at least one shelf for books in each of the children's rooms or in the family room. Put books for younger children on the lower shelves, within easy reach so they will also feel included.

Number of Volumes   This is a personal choice, of course. But you could start by focusing on the interests of each family member. Find out what their preferences are. Then stock up on books that will draw them to the "library." You can begin with a few representative books and add to the collection over time. For easy access, group together books on related subjects—science, novels, picture books, reference, self-help, and so on. Make sure there are a few titles for every member of the family.

Options and Additions

If you wish to simplify further, here are a couple of ideas that do not require a particular skill such as carpentry. Even the youngest member of your family can participate in assembling these book storage units.

Brick Blocks   Purchase bricks or concrete blocks at a hardware or home maintenance store. Set down two to four blocks and lay a colorful board across the top. Display your books and hold them in place with two bricks as bookends.

Crate Cases   Buy plastic crates at any multi-purpose store or pick up a couple of discarded wooden orange crates from a local supermarket. Paint or use as they are. They are sturdy and childproof and provide easy access to books.

Card Catalog   Create a filing system (filing box with index cards and dividers available at stationery or office supply stores). Label the dividers according to the type of books found in your home library—mysteries, poetry, science, fiction, and so on. As you and your children read, write a short evaluation of the book on the index card and file it. This card will provide useful tips to other family members who might be interested in reading the same book at another time.

Homemade Books   Encourage your children to write their own books, to design a cover and to add illustrations. Bind them with ribbon, poster board, construction paper, and ribbons or staples. Add these books to the family collection. Make some extra ones to give as gifts.

Bookmarks   Keep a supply of colorful bookmarks in a cup or small box. You can acquire free ones from most bookstore sales clerks. But encourage your children to make their own as well, using construction paper, cardboard, stickers, and markers.

Acquire Library Cards

When children are old enough to sign their names, take them to the public library and help them apply for their own library card. Of course, you can borrow books for them on your card, but it's not the same! I remember the day my children received their very own cards. This event was an important milestone for them and for me—just as important as the day we bought their first bicycle, skateboard, or ballet slippers. A personal library card is an effective way to introduce your children to books. And the benefits are more far-reaching than you may realize.

Increased Awareness   Children become more aware of what a visit to the library involves. Having their own cards provides a new access to the books they want to read. It gives them a sense of purpose.

Greater Interest   Children with library cards usually take more interest in the library itself and how it works. They discover the many ways a library can be useful to people of all ages. They ask questions, explore the shelves more eagerly, and notice what is available for reference as well as for pleasure.

More Respect   Most parents want to foster in their children respect for books and for the written word. I believe that boys and girls with library privileges will cultivate this respect more easily than those who do not have a card of their own. They realize they are borrowing something that must be returned. Library books are like a renewable gift. You can always have more. And you have the joy and privilege of selecting them yourself.

Heightened Sense of Responsibility A card holder must bring the books home, take care of them, and return them on time in good condition. I found that my children paid more attention to the due date when they were responsible for their own books. We marked the date together on the calendar. They knew how much time they had to read their books. And they looked forward to the next visit when they could trade in what they'd read for a new stack.

Visit the Library Regularly

 When your children have their own cards, take them to the library often. If you can go every week or two, wonderful! Set aside a few minutes during each visit to introduce them to a new part of the library.

Reference Section   If one of your children has to do a report on birds, show her the reference shelves. Point out the various anthologies and encyclopedias that have material on birds. Show her the difference between a reference book—one that must remain in the library for all users—and books on the study of birds (ornithology) in the science section that she can check out and take home.

Card Catalog   Show your children how to look up a particular book by title, subject, or author. Many libraries today have the data on computer or other electronic device. If your library offers a variety of options, point out all of them.

Book Stacks   Walk down the aisles and peruse the books. Help your children compare the data on the file or card with the information on the spine of the book. Look for a particular book together so your children will know how and where to make a specific choice.

A Bit of History   If you know the information and are comfortable talking with children, consider giving a group of kids a tour of the library. Explain the history behind cataloging books according to the Dewey decimal system. Ask them questions about how they might organize a library, what to do with old titles, and how to keep up with new ones released each year.

The Librarian   Perhaps a librarian would be willing to speak with your children for a few moments to answer any questions they may have, to take them on a brief tour behind the scenes, and to talk about a librarian's job.

Related Services   Most large public libraries, and even some smaller ones, now have many book-related products and services. For example, you can borrow long-playing records, CDs, videos, computer games, and audio cassettes. Some libraries, such as the San Diego Public Library in San Diego, California, feature an art film or other presentation once a month. Book fairs to raise money for library improvements, puppet shows for children, summer reading contests, holiday programs, and much more are all available throughout most library systems. Encourage your children to discover and use these various options that are designed to introduce people to books in ways they may not have thought of before.

Visit Children's Bookstores

Today there are around three hundred children's bookstores across the United States. Less than a decade ago there were fewer than five. Children's books have grown in volume and in popularity—so much so that many chain bookstores have large sections devoted to children's titles. Some stores focus exclusively on children's books.

Boys and girls will love a visit to such a store. Many are equipped with tables and chairs for the younger crowd, a toy box, and a selection of books to enjoy while browsing. Some stores feature special book signings with children's authors. Children can meet the authors and purchase an autographed copy of one of their books.

Some children's bookstores also provide support materials for young readers, such as audio and videotapes, puppets, coloring and activity books, educational workbooks, and books on tape.

Visiting a children's bookstore is another of the most effective ways to introduce children to books and to help them become familiar with all that books have to offer.

Plenty to Choose From

Baby Books   For the infant to toddler-aged child. Usually colorful soft or hardcover books made of sturdy nontoxic material are perfect first books.

Picture Books and Concept Books   For children two through six years of age. A wide variety is available in both fiction and nonfiction, concept and fantasy, ABC and animal books, most with large, full-color illustrations to engage the reader as well as the listener. Ask the bookseller for her or his favorites and for some examples of books that have won the Caldecott Medal, awarded annually for best illustration of a children's book.

Beginning Readers   Designed for children who are learning to read, these books provide stimulating stories and interesting nonfiction topics that will interest the five- to eight-year-old reader. Vocabulary for such books is generally appropriate for the youngest readers. Some publishers that specialize in beginning readers include HarperCollins, Dial, Bantam, Macmillan, and Random House.

Storybooks   The storybook, unlike the picture book, focuses on the story rather than the pictures and is supported with a few color or black-and-white illustrations. Storybooks may be suitable for a child to read to himself, but they may be more challenging for the beginning reader. Storybooks are of interest to children aged six to nine and sometimes older.

Chapter Books   Children in the middle grades are generally ready to read a full-length story. They like the continuity of one long story that spans sixty pages or more. And they enjoy reading what has the look and feel or composition of a book for older readers. Publishers have responded to this interest with what is called the "chapter book," a story that is broken up into six to eight chapters. Such books are generally published in series. The famous Baby-Sitters series by Ann Martin is a good example of popular chapter books.

Novels and Information Books   Such books are available on a wide variety of topics of interest to ten-year-olds and up.

Some titles are specifically geared to adolescents or young adults. A bookseller can help your children locate titles that are right for them.

Many stores also schedule story hours, puppet shows, author visits, holiday promotionals, and sales, and they may publish a monthly or quarterly newsletter for their customers.

To locate children's bookstores in your neighborhood or city, look in the Yellow Pages of your phone directory. For more information about children's bookstores as a business, contact:

Association of Booksellers for Children
National Office
4412 Chowen Ave. So., #303
Minneapolis, MN 55410
1-800-421-1665
(612) 926-6650

Memberships are also available on three different levels. If you are interested, contact the main office listed above. New members receive a packet of sample materials and information about book publishing, as well as a quarterly newsletter, *Building Blocks*.

Build a Basic Book Collection

Another way to hook your kids on books is to build a basic book collection together. Create or set aside a shelf to hold books that everyone in the family can enjoy. Here are some ideas to consider when compiling your selection.

Reference Books A dictionary, a Bible, and a one-volume or multi-volume set of encyclopedias that is suitable for children. *World Book* is a trusted name. We have enjoyed using it in our home for more than twenty years. But there are others. I encourage you to conduct your own research before making this large investment. A book of quotations, such as *Bartlett's*, is useful, as well as an almanac, a general science book, and a medical reference book.

Classics You may wish to add some of your favorite books of poetry. Emily Dickinson and Eve Merriam, among others, come to mind. *Winnie-the-Pooh, Peter Rabbit,* and *The Velveteen Rabbit* may be titles that you'd like your children to be familiar with. For older readers, consider *Little Women* and *Little Men, A Christmas Carol* and other works by Dickens, and the Little House books by Laura Ingalls Wilder, to name a few.

Childhood Favorites I kept a few of my favorites on hand even after I became a mother, so that I could share them with my children. Perhaps you have some of your own books still in a box or trunk. Or perhaps a parent or other relative has them stored for you, as my mother did for a time. Bring them out, set them on the shelf, and read them with your children. It's a wonderful way to link the generations and to introduce your children to books that may be new to them. Some of mine include traditional favorites such as *The Little House, Geraldine Belinda Marybelle Scott, The Hundred Dresses,* and *Little Women.*

Special Books   As your children take increasing interest in reading and getting acquainted with authors and their books, you may wish to encourage them to collect books of their own. Not just any books, but special ones—books that relate to their interests, hobbies, and curiosities.

For example, when my daughter Julie was in elementary school, she collected the Winnie-the-Pooh series and the books in the Little House series by Laura Ingalls Wilder. My son enjoyed sports novels by Matt Christopher. And my younger daughter liked stories by Carolyn Haywood and Beverly Cleary.

What are your children interested in? You might help them build a collection of science books, novels by a favorite author, books about birds or flowers, sports books, mysteries, or books about cars or computers or poetry.

Add to the collection with gifts for birthdays and holidays. Spread the word among family and friends as well. Or give your children money to purchase books that will fill out their collection.

One woman I know became interested in cooking and nutrition when she was in high school. She began buying books on these subjects and now has an impressive library. What started as a hobby and keen interest is now her profession. She teaches cooking classes and has become a respected authority on organic food and healthful food preparation in the city where she lives.

Choosing Books for Specific Age Groups

Approximately sixty thousand books for children and young people are currently in print, according to a parent reading guide published by Reading Is Fundamental. What a selection!

Reviews and recommendations can guide you, but don't discount your instincts. Trust your own sense of what is appropriate for your children's needs and interests at their different stages in life. Here are some guidelines for the various age groups.

Babies and Toddlers   ABC books featuring familiar objects and people (parents, siblings, other babies, toys, and pets) are favorites, as well as stories using simple vocabulary. Poems, nursery rhymes, and books with lots of sensory detail help your little ones learn to identify the five senses and relate them to the world around them.

Preschoolers   Stories about their environment and everyday experiences appeal to this age group. They especially like stories featuring animal characters or children of preschool age, stories with plenty of action, simple language and concepts they can grasp easily, such as playing with friends, birthday parties, holiday celebrations, and books with humor, surprise, and wonder—all with plenty of illustrations.

Young Readers   Children in this age group enjoy stories with oft-repeated words and phrases, simple sentences, familiar vocabulary, realistic children of their age dealing with life experiences and feelings that readers can relate to, craft and recipe books, simple science concepts, books about animals, simple mysteries, and, of course, humor.

Middle Graders and Preteens   As children grow up they look for books with information about subjects that interest them, collections of fascinating facts, humor, stories about

19

relationships and friendships between peers and family members, biographies written for their age group, mysteries, science fiction, books that feature characters they can relate to in situations at home and in school, and stories set in other countries and other times.

Books open the way to learning—a way that could provide a seed of inspiration that will inspire a young person to pursue a profession, career, or satisfying hobby.

Teens and Young Adults By this age it's best to let your sons and daughters choose their own reading material. To discover what that is, go to a bookstore with them and talk as you browse together. Give them some time alone, as well, to make choices without your influence. You might even give them some money to spend on a book or two of their choice.

The best example for your teens is to let them see you reading for enjoyment and for information. Acknowledge your teens' interests and ask them for suggestions as to what books they would like to receive or collect. If they experience a lull in reading interest, look the other way. They are likely to return to books if they have developed an appreciation of them and grown up in a home where reading and books are valued.

Display Book Posters

 My grandchildren's bedroom walls are decorated with posters of children's books. You may wish to do the same in your children's rooms or in the family or recreation room in your home. It's another good way to surround your children with books. Such posters also make unique and thoughtful gifts. Where can you purchase them?

Book Publishers Contact the publicity or public relations department of any major children's book publisher and inquire about posters. You may be able to get posters of some of your favorite titles. A reference book called *Writer's Market,* found in libraries and sold in some bookstores, lists several hundred book publishing companies and provides the phone number, fax number, and address of each one.

Art Stores and Museums I found some wonderful posters at The Children's Bookshop in The Metropolitan Museum of Art in New York. You might also check stores and museums in your community. You can frame them if you wish, as I did, or hang them up with thumbtacks or double-stick tape as my daughter did for her children. They are inexpensive, fun to look at, colorful, and an easy way to decorate walls. You can change them easily too.

Children's Book Council For information about posters,

bookmarks, and other learning materials related to current and past books, contact this organization:

The Children's Book Council
Room 404
568 Broadway
New York, NY 10012

You can join their mailing list to stay informed on a quarterly basis. This is also a good source of information about the children's book industry, authors and illustrators, and promotions related to children's books. For example, a recent Children's Book Council (CBC) catalog included a list of CBC Member Publishers that showed what materials they have available to the public. In a quick study of this simple catalog, an individual can easily assess what he or she would like to order. The list includes:

Where you get it	*What you get*	*What you send to get it*
name of publisher	item available	postage and envelope size

The CBC is a good source of this and other information on many aspects of children's publishing.

Create
a Reading
Corner

Imagine this: A corner of a child's room bounded by a colorful area rug piled high with soft, plush pillows or a comfortable beanbag chair. A nearby shelf or children's table holds an assortment of wonderful books—storybooks, picture books, beginning readers, concept books, ABC books—all kinds of books to intrigue and satisfy almost any child. Put a child in the picture, and you have a reading corner that will provide hours of education and entertainment. You could add an audio cassette player for children to enjoy books that come with tapes.

For Adolescents and Teens Put them in charge of their own space. Give them a decorating allowance as an incentive. They might want to purchase a futon, beanbag chair, or floor cushions for seating. Some of these items can be found at a garage sale, swap meet, or at a used furniture or discount store for a reasonable price. Book posters, a simple book shelf and plenty of books, an audio cassette or CD player might be included—depending on the person, the space, and funds available.

A Place for the Whole Family If you have a recreation or family room, you may wish to create a reading corner for the whole family to enjoy. One or more persons could share the space. Spread cushions and pillows on the floor or place a comfortable old sofa against one wall with a table to prop up feet. Add bookshelves or just set out a big basket with magazines, books, newspapers, newsletters, and other reading material. Family members can dip into the common pile or bring their own book or magazine. You could even hang a sign on the wall that lets visitors know that this is a special place—for people and books: "Shh! Readers at work!" or "Please don't disturb. I'm lost in a good book!"

There isn't any *one* way to create a reading corner. Make it personal. Make it comfortable. Make it appealing—but make it! It's another way to introduce your kids to books and reading—and to keep the relationship alive.

Tour a Book Publishing Company

If you live in or near a large city, it should be fairly easy to locate a publishing company. If you live in a rural area or small town you may be able to find a small publishing or printing company within a short distance. Check the Yellow Pages of your telephone directory or inquire at your local library. It may be possible to receive a tour of the facility. This would be a great field trip for a group of students or Scouts.

Observing the publishing process firsthand is an effective way to introduce children and young people to books and reading. If you cannot visit a publishing company in person, you can still take a tour by means of a book about publishing or by doing a research project about the process. Publishing houses may have educational information available for the asking. Contact the public relations department of a particular company. Addresses are available in the reference book *Writer's Market,* available at the library, in bookstores, or directly from F & W Publications, 1507 Dana Ave., Cincinnati, OH 45207.

Following are some elements of the publishing business that you may want to read about so your children will receive maximum benefit from the experience.

Types of Publishing This includes *trade-book publishing,* a term used for books of a general nature (biography, how-to, cookbooks, history, travel, current affairs, novels for children and adults) sold mainly through bookstores or book departments of other stores; *paper-bound books,* the production of small-sized, brightly covered paperback editions, often reprints of higher-priced, hardcover books; *textbook publishing,* which accounts for the largest area of publishing, including school and college books and workbooks; *subscription book publishing,* involving the distribution of books through salespeople who sell directly to book buyers in homes, libraries, schools, colleges, training facilities, and other places; and *specialized publishing,* including the production of business, technical, scientific, medical, and law books for students and professional people in specific fields of work.

Careers in Publishing Writers, editors, researchers, illustrators, proofreaders, press operators, computer programmers, typesetters, graphic artists, and book binders are some of the people who have a career in publishing. Salespeople and those in advertising and promotion play an important role in book production as well. Literary agents and librarians are also related to the book industry. Agents help writers find an appropriate publisher for their work, and librarians often help writers and publishers in researching material needed for the publication of books. And, of course, after the books are published and on the library shelves, a good librarian will encourage people to read the various books he or she has purchased.

Tell Stories

 Families have told stories for generations—to entertain, to foster values, to share traditions, and to express feelings. Today literacy specialists encourage us to tell stories for an additional reason—in order to support the development of reading and writing in our children.

The simple act of storytelling can help them:

- experience language in colorful ways
- expand their vocabulary
- express their individual creativity
- exercise their ability to share ideas with others
- extend their interest in books

Choose a Time

Holidays and Special Events These are ideal occasions to participate in and learn about ethnic and religious traditions.

Bedtime This is a favorite time of closeness between parents and children. Use stories to quell fears, prepare children for sleep, and reassure them.

Waiting Rooms While waiting for a doctor or dentist, or in line at the grocery store or post office, make up stories about the situation you're in—a great way to teach your children new words and give them a new experience.

Car, Bus, Train, or Plane   Travel often produces wiggly children. Reading to them helps settle them down and passes the time in a productive and creative way. Weave a story about the surroundings and about your destination.

Choose a Story

Stories are all around us. Pick a tale from your own life, your family's history, or your own imagination.

Family History   Your children can discover some wonderful folklore and folk tales from your heritage. You may uncover real-life stories or fantasies that are part of your ethnic background. Your children will also enjoy the true stories you tell about their early life or about your family before they were born.

Your Children   Weave a story with your children as the central characters, using familiar events and friends and experiences from their lives. They'll squeal with delight. This is also a great way to celebrate their accomplishments—first day at school, learning to ride a bike, receiving an award.

Current Events   Look for stories in the news. You may read about a heroic child or a boy or girl who has achieved some recognition or a humorous tale about a child and a pet. Paraphrase these stories from the news, and encourage a discussion with your children.

Memorabilia   Build a story around an object or photo that triggers a memory for you. Perhaps your children would enjoy a story about a favorite book you still have in your library or the background on a family heirloom you have on display.

Add-on Story   Here each member of the family adds a line to a story one person starts. The result can be surprising and usually quite humorous. And it keeps everyone paying attention. Good for the driver too!

Choose a Presentation Style

The *way* you tell a story is just as important—sometimes more so—as the story itself. Following are some things you can do to grab and hold your young readers' interest.

Fit Your Story to the Audience Consider the age and attention span and interests of your listeners.

Use Body Language Act out the story as you go along, making use of hand gestures, eye and body movement, and changes of voice inflection.

Engage the Listeners Children love to participate. They can clap their hands or repeat a certain word on cue. Ask questions to get them thinking. What should Hansel and Gretel do? What would you do if you were Carl the dog or Harry the monkey?

Use Hand Props Wear a funny hat. Throw on a towel for a cape. Set up a doll or stuffed animal. Pantomime actions. Use stick or paper bag puppets. Choose whatever will enliven and dramatize the story to enrich the experience for your listeners.

As your children become familiar with storytelling, they will soon want to tell stories of their own. Encourage them to each take a turn, and you be the audience. From that point on, the bridge to books will be easy to cross together.

PART 2

Encourage Reading

Reward Individual Reading

When my children were in elementary school, my husband and I instituted a new house rule: no TV on school nights and a limited amount on weekends. The kids didn't like it at first, but after a few weeks everyone agreed that our home was more peaceful, more fun, and more intimate. The children did their homework without prodding. They read more books, and we talked more as a family.

Turning off the television can do more to stimulate reading than any other thing I can think of. To encourage my children to read books, I also created a reward system. They could stay up a half-hour past their usual bedtime *if* they used the time to read. They didn't have to stay up to read, but if they wanted to, they could have the extra time. Before long everyone was involved in a book, then another and another. We took more trips to the library than usual, and as a result we discovered authors and titles we had never known.

When it comes to encouraging your children to read, consider a reward system. It works, especially with younger boys and girls. Here are some ways to reward the readers in your home.

Hats Off to You Hang a piece of poster board on a wall in your home. Cut out various kinds of hats from magazine and newspaper ads, or draw and cut them out of colored construction paper. Put them in a box near the poster board or pin them to the bottom of the board. Place each child's name in a list on the board. Each time a child completes a book, ask him or her to share something from the book with the family. Then print the name of the book on the paper hat and pin the hat to the board next to that child's name.

As a child fills up the space next to her name she may receive a special treat—such as a meal out or a favorite dessert. Or you could have an additional box filled with homemade coupons good for certain benefits or services. As a child fills up the spaces on the chart, she may choose a coupon. There is no competition in this. Each one can proceed at her or his own pace. When the chart is filled, make a new one or try some other approach to keep your kids hooked on books.

A Snicker of Acknowledgment   A friend of mine who was a public speaker kept a bag of miniature Snickers candy bars with her wherever she traveled. To encourage her audience to participate in her talks and to discuss their experiences, she would hold up a candy bar and say, "Anyone who shares or participates will receive a Snicker of encouragement."

This custom became such a part of her presentation that people all over the country came to expect Ruth's bag of Snickers as an important part of her visit.

You might do something similar with your young readers. Reward their individual reading with a "snicker" of acknowledgment (Snickers bars), or some variation thereof. Examples: a "slice" (apples or chewing gum); "wedge" (oranges); "cup" (favorite beverage), and so on. Or give your children a choice of the options you offer. The item, of course, isn't as important as what it represents.

Treasure (or Treat) Bag   Collect small favors and treats as rewards for individual reading. Look for little "loot" at garage sales, close-outs, the 99-cent stores now open in many cities, thrift shops, and resale boutiques. Keep these items on hand, ready to dispense when a child shows you his or her completed book.

By the time children are in upper elementary grades, the reward system may not be important to them, or may no longer be appropriate. But by then they will have acquired the habit of reading, and the reading itself will be its own reward.

Read Books as a Family

 One young mother by the name of Nancy said one of her fondest memories of childhood was of her family reading together. After dinner each night her mother and father took turns reading a chapter of a book that everyone could enjoy. Favorites included *Where the Red Fern Grows, Little Women, Julie of the Wolves, The Summer of My German Soldier,* and others. As they got older, not everyone was home at the same time, but the tradition continued. Whoever gathered at the appointed time read together. Latecomers could catch up on their own since the book was always available on the kitchen table.

When they traveled by car or plane for family vacations, reading was part of that experience as well. Older children read to younger ones, or parents read aloud and everyone listened. Today, Nancy, a mother of three children under ten, carries on the same tradition in her home. They are reading some of the same books she loved as a child, as well as new ones that are favorites of her children.

You may feel too busy to read as a family. Or perhaps you and your family members are going in many different directions— sports, piano lessons, community and church services. Nancy says her family has similar demands. This is their solution:

1. They make reading a priority in their home.
2. They hang a master calendar in the kitchen where all outside commitments are posted for everyone to see.
3. They select one fifteen-minute segment each day when everyone can be together. Generally, it follows a family meal. They plan to adjust this routine as required as the children get older.
4. They take turns reading. If the text from the selected book is too difficult for some, they listen. At the end of the time together, the younger family members may read a poem or a selection from a book of their choice as their contribution.

Nancy says that all of her children are eager and excellent readers. And she and her husband have noticed an increased intimacy in their family life as a result of this special time spent together.

If you would like to try this in your home, here are some guidelines that may be helpful in getting started.

- Call a family meeting and discuss the possibility.
- Start with those who express interest.
- Pick a time—once a day, once a week, or whatever your family agrees on.
- Keep one another accountable. Let children know that it's not okay to skip the reading time unless they let a parent know ahead of time and agree to make up the missed pages on their own.
- Plan a reading-related outing after finishing each book. You might visit a museum, library, garden, historical house, national monument, national park, or a new city as it relates to the story or topic you've read about. One family, for example, read *Anne of Green Gables*, by L. M. Montgomery, and then visited Prince Edward Island, Canada, the setting for the story and the birthplace of the author.

- Give older children opportunities to contribute as readers, book choosers, outing planners, and so on.
- Provide settings where growing readers can use the information gained from books: cooking, gardening, science experiments, crafts, art projects, etc.

Create Reading Partnerships

Here's another way to encourage reading. Pair up the readers in the family: parent and child, older and younger siblings, reader and pre-reader. You can put a chart showing the partnerships and reading times on a bulletin board in the family room or on the refrigerator in the kitchen. Change partnerships each week or month, or whatever suits your family.

For example, seven-year-old John can pair up with four-year-old Matt. John agrees to read one short book, chapter, or story (appropriate for his reading level) to Matt each day or a couple of times a week. John gets practice reading, and Matt gets the benefit of a story, as well as the example of his older brother mastering a book. John may even teach Matt a few simple words from the book, and each time they come up in the story, Matt can pronounce them, which allows him to be involved in an active way.

Mom could partner with John and read a story that he is interested in but can't yet read on his own. John gets some private time with Mom and also the pleasure of being read to.

Mom and Dad can be a team as well. I know one couple who read to each other every night before going to sleep. They take turns reading chapters of a favorite novel—several pages a night until the book is complete. Janice says it's one of their very special times together as a couple. "We have discovered that reading together promotes intimacy and communication," she said. "So much conversation is stimulated as a result of reading to one another."

Children who are close in age can also be reading partners. Even though they can read by themselves, a new world of sharing and caring opens up when two people share the joy of a book together. They learn to cooperate (by choosing a book of mutual interest). They learn about each other's interests. They learn how to support each other's reading development.

Reading partners can also help one another with homework reading, quizzes on reading comprehension, and vocabulary drills. This is also an opportunity for family members to become better acquainted and to create caring relationships.

Learn about the Origin of a Book or Story

Children are often curious about how authors get their ideas and what motivated them to write certain stories. For example, Beverly Cleary based many of her books, such as *Ramona the Pest,* on the lives and people in her own family and neighborhood.

You can help motivate and inspire your children to read and perhaps to keep a diary of their own experiences and feelings by encouraging them to find out the background of some of their favorite stories. Here are some ways to do that.

1. Contact the public relations department of the publisher of a book you want to know more about. Many publishers have information sheets on their authors.
2. Write to a particular author and ask about the origin of a specific book. If you don't have access to his or her home address, send your letter in care of the publisher. Company addresses are listed in *Writer's Market,* found in the reference section of most libraries.
3. Attend author fairs and book signings in your community. Personal contact with children's book writers is the best way to find the information you want.

For example, at a recent author's fair in San Diego, the coordinator compiled a booklet entitled *Meet the Authors.* She invited each guest author to contribute information about his or her work and life. Following are some examples.

Larry Dane Brimner sometimes looks at events from his own childhood for inspiration for his stories. *Elliot Fry's Good-Bye* (Boyds Mills Press) is loosely based on his one experience with running away.

Fire Mate is author Olga Cossi's favorite of all her books. "It tells more about me than any other story I have written," she says. "It is about my love of animals and my American Indian connection."

Kathryn Hewitt says that she grew up in a family where the children were encouraged to read. Her father kept the shelves overflowing with books, and her mother often read to the family and told stories of the "old country" (Ukraine) where she was born. Kathryn's love of folk tales began with these stories, and now some of her writing includes retold tales from other countries.

Ramon Royal Ross says he writes stories that reflect the Walla Walla Valley, located in the southeastern corner of Washington state, during the middle of the twentieth century when he was a boy. But most important, he says, are the characters he creates who share the things that all human beings have in common: "the need for a sense of worth, and acceptance, and love, and family."

Most of my early children's books came directly out of my relationship with my children. I wrote a book on tennis when my son and I were avid players. I wrote two books on horses during the time my youngest daughter owned a horse. And I wrote books on ways kids could earn money and entertain based on my oldest daughter's interests at that time.

4. Report on the life of an author. As you learn the background of favorite stories, you will probably want to learn more about the lives of the writers themselves. The lives of several twentieth-century children's authors—living and deceased—are in book form, and you can locate them at the library.

- Jim Henson of Sesame Street fame
- Laura Ingalls Wilder
- Pearl Buck
- Willa Cather

Ask your librarian for further help.

In addition, you can read brief biographical sketches of children's writers in such reference books as *Something About the Author, Who's Who,* and other compilations at the library. This information may also be available through computer services.

Organize an Author Fair

Many schools and reading organizations across the United States, as well as children's bookstores, provide access to authors and their books through an author or book fair.

For example, in San Diego, where I live, the county school district hosts an annual Authors' Fair each spring. Authors from the area and students from county schools meet at the district education office. Authors conduct thirty-minute presentations to various groups, closing with a question and answer session. Then boys and girls and their teachers tour the all-purpose room where book-related art projects decorate the walls and tables. They are eager to find their school, their classroom, their individual book-related artwork. It's an exciting time for everyone. Meeting and talking with a "real live author" is an event children will never forget. Nor will the authors. I speak from experience!

If there is an annual author fair in your area, consider getting involved. If none exists, you may wish to organize one or ask the librarian at your children's school to host such an event. The following guidelines may be helpful.

Select an Author (or Authors)   Choose your author(s) as you would any professional (doctor, attorney, consultant). Inquire at your library or local reading association for the names of local children's writers, or contact an author through the publisher. Call the publicity department and ask for information about individuals and availability. If possible, speak with the author on the phone and, if possible, sit in on one of his or her presentations. Don't assume that because a person can write he or she can also speak well. You will want an author who can connect with the children in a memorable way.

Settle on a Fee Contact the author's publishing company first, or talk with other groups who have hired the author so you will know what fees to expect. Parent-teacher groups and school and library budgets are often limited. But for such an occasion, you may be able to garner additional money through a fund for special events or by asking a local merchant to become a sponsor or by holding a bake sale to raise enough for the author's visit. Keep in mind that an author is a free-lance worker whose fee must justify a day away from his primary source of income—writing. Also the payment is usually in addition to travel and lodging expenses. Some publishers provide transportation. Others do not. Inquire about this in the beginning. A flat fee that includes money for expenses may be appropriate. Or the author may prefer to submit an invoice for expenses following the presentation.

Choose a Date Planning is a must, since many authors are booked as far ahead as a year. Check the community, library, or school calendar first, and then contact the selected author or his publicist with a choice of dates. Allow enough time so that the children can prepare for the visit by reading some of the author's books, making book-related art projects, or writing out questions they want to ask.

Have Books Available It is important to have the author's books available. Authors come not to put on a performance but rather to talk about the process of writing. Students who are unprepared miss out on an exciting and informative experience, and authors end up feeling they have wasted their time.

Circulate some books before the author's visit and then have additional copies on hand for students to purchase, though no child or parent should feel any pressure to buy a book. Include time for autographing, or ask the author to sign a piece of paper that can be copied, cut into bookmark size, and distributed to each child following the visit.

Create a Realistic Schedule   To receive the best the author has to offer, set up the day to include ample breaks—time for rest, food, and water. And be sure to consult the author about his or her preferences for group size, location, and other logistics. For example, when I speak I prefer to meet with two classes of the same grade in the library or multi-purpose room rather than making the rounds to each individual classroom. If possible, bring the students to the author rather than asking the author to walk from one location to another.

Also consider the type of books and the intended age group the author focuses on. Some specialize in picture books. Others write young adult novels or non-fiction books for middle-grade readers. That information will help you target the student audience. Kindergartners, for example, would not be interested in hearing about writing mysteries for teens. And sixth graders probably would not care to listen to a picture book writer.

If the author has written for a wide range of readers, consider two large assemblies—one for the primary grades and one for the upper-grade students. I believe the large groups are less effective, however, because they do not offer the intimacy and personal connection that smaller groups do.

These are some of the things to consider when planning. The authors can help you with this, so don't hesitate to ask for their advice and preferences.

Follow Up   You may wish to set aside some time at the end of the day for a brief meeting. The author will appreciate "putting his feet up" for a few moments. This is an opportunity to discuss the day's results, to answer any questions left unaddressed, and to provide the payment. If you cannot pay the author that day, let him or her know that ahead of time, so it does not come as a surprise.

You may wish to write to the publisher to let a public relations representative know how the visit went. The author would probably appreciate hearing from you as well. The children may wish to write a thank-you note, but they should realize that the author is unlikely to respond to all of them individually.

Plan Another Author Fair As soon as this one is successfully behind you, you may wish to consider planning another. Invite new people to join you, or turn over the reins to one of your committee persons. By then you will be a pro—able to perform many of the tasks with ease. And, no doubt, you will also receive some helpful advice from the author you recently featured and suggestions and preferences from students and teachers as to who and what they would like the next time.

Create a Book-Buying Fund

Regina, a mother of three children of elementary school age, remembers her mother providing money in her budget for books. "They were a priority in our home," she said, holding up one treasure she had saved through the years.

Leonard, a father and schoolteacher, had a different experience. He said that books were a low priority in his family, so it was out of the question to ask to buy a book. "I used the library, of course. But sometimes I wanted to buy a copy of a special book so I wouldn't have to give it back. I think it's important for kids to *own* some books. I've made a point of buying books for my children and giving them money for birthdays and holidays to be used to purchase a book."

I agree with Leonard. My parents allowed me to buy books, some of which I still have today. When my children were growing up, I encouraged them to purchase at least a couple of books each year. By the time my oldest daughter was in high school, she had a nice collection of some of her favorite books for young people.

If you would like to initiate a book-buying fund in your family, here are some options for getting it off the ground.

Open a Special Savings Account Every member of the family can contribute something to this account—money earned at work, or from part-time jobs such as newspaper deliveries, baby-sitting, lawn mowing, and so on. Naturally, the parents contribute the most—whatever sum they agree upon based on their household spending plan—and should be on hand to help their children make wise choices. Some of the money could be put toward books the entire family will read, such as encyclopedias, Bibles, dictionaries, and other large items. And some of the money can be divided up over the year for individual purchases.

Appoint a Bookkeeper A parent or responsible teen could serve as bookkeeper, noting the date of purchase, book title, price, and family member who made the purchase. This method will keep the fund available to everyone. You may establish a set amount of money for each person to use as he or she wishes (with some guidance, of course), or individuals can dip into the fund (with permission) when they wish to make a purchase.

Some family members may be more interested in books than others and may ask for more than what seems their fair share. By keeping a ledger, each one can see at a glance what is available. Two or more can also combine their portion to buy a mutually beneficial book, or they may wish to trade their allotment for something else.

There is no one way to establish or administer the funds. You may have a better system than the one mentioned here. What matters is that you let your children know that reading is important and that money for books does have a place in your family spending plan.

"Watch" a Book— "Listen" to a Book

Even before my oldest grandson was able to read, his mother introduced him to books on audiotape. Travel by car provided a great opportunity for extended exposure to a good story in this way. Some weekend evenings were set aside to watch a book on videotape. *The Secret Garden, Where the Red Fern Grows,* and *Charlotte's Web* are among their favorites.

I don't believe that cassette tapes should take the place of reading, but they are a wonderful supplement to the written word, extending and encouraging the reading experience.

You may wish to read the book first as a family and then watch the video presentation together or listen to the audio version. To get the most out of either experience, consider the following:

1. *Choose a story that appears in book and cassette format.*
   Many publishers now present the book and cassette as a package. Inquire at your bookstore.
2. *Read the book first.*
   Introduce your children to the published book, then look for a movie or video tie-in, if available.
3. *Discuss the story to stimulate thought and participation.*
   Ask your children to review the book and to discuss what they liked and didn't like. Then compare the book to the video or movie version.

4. *Learn something interesting about the author, the setting, or the era of the story.*

     Do some informal, story-related research before or after reading the book.
5. *Write a short book review or report, and share it with a friend, school class, or family member.*
6. *Record your children's voices as they read or tell a favorite story.*

Cassette tapes and movies are wonderful ways to extend and amplify the reading experience.

Use Books for Planning Vacations

 For the MacKenzie family, one of the highlights of their year is deciding on a time and place for their vacation. Because they are enthusiastic about books, they use them extensively as part of their vacation planning process.

One year they learned about the life and times of the Shakers through a book one of their children used for a history project at school. So they included a side trip to Shakertown, Kentucky, to visit the historical buildings, view the furniture, and sample foods from the Shaker era.

Another year they visited southern California, where they spent a day at Disneyland and toured Universal Studios and the set for the television show "Star Trek" after reading books about special effects in filmmaking.

A trip to Washington, D.C., made an ideal vacation spot after reading about the White House, the Washington Monument, the Lincoln Memorial, and the Vietnam War Memorial.

The MacKenzies also use travel books to plan their itinerary, including stops along the way at unique restaurants and local parks, historic houses, museums, or other local places of interest. While visiting new places, they generally buy a book about the town or community to add to their collection. Even the youngest child remembers facts and bits of information that would impress any adult.

Here are some ways to extend your reading experiences to your family vacation, day jaunts, or weekend trips, depending, of course, on available funds and time and location.

1. Visit the real-life setting of a favorite book.

    Example: Mansfield, Missouri, for the Little House books by Laura Ingalls Wilder

2. Visit the birthplace of a book character or person of historical significance.

    Example: Philadelphia, Pennsylvania, for the home of Betsy Ross

3. Visit cities famous for certain monuments or ethnic groups or historical significance.

    Example: San Diego, San Juan Capistrano for the California missions

4. Visit a national park and learn about its unique characteristics:

    Example: Yellowstone National Park

5. Visit a planetarium, garden, museum, concert hall, television or movie studio, university campus, athletic stadium, or government building in your community or nearby city after reading a book about the place itself or the subject associated with it.

While you drive or fly or travel by plane or bus, include reading as part of the trip. As a family, you could read one of the books that relates to your destination, or individuals can read to themselves and then discuss what they learned during a meal or while riding or driving. This will enrich the experience for everyone—readers and even those too young to read.

Share Bedtime Stories

 Consider making bedtime stories a family affair. Choose favorite stories that appeal to everyone. Poetry, Bible stories, picture books, short novels, and others will then be accessible to all. As younger children grow, they will follow the custom, perhaps choosing the book if they can't yet read, and then picking up the lead when they are of reading age by reading to a younger sibling.

You might also include books on tape, lullaby tapes, spiritual songs, and stories based on Scripture as part of the bedtime ritual.

At night it is probably best to stay away from anything too stimulating or scary such as mysteries or ghost stories. But almost anything else is appropriate, as long as you approve of it and your children enjoy it. You can provide a good mix through the year, so boys and girls will be exposed to lyrics, poetry, fiction, Bible stories, biographies, and whatever else appeals to them.

It is unlikely that everyone will be able to read together at the same time, but over a week or two plan at least a few evenings when your whole family can enjoy some bedtime reading together—even if the actual bedtimes vary.

If you wish to make it even more special, add an unexpected treat once a week—such as homemade cookies and a drink while listening to a story, or a bubble bath for the younger set as you read to them, or a book and a tape after they crawl under the covers. Make up your own customs.

Offer your children some choices. Ask what they like best. Depending on their ages, you may create a variety of traditions that change as they grow up. The important thing is not so much what you do or how you do it, but that you do *something* meaningful to encourage reading and togetherness.

Organize a Reading Party

You may have organized a birthday party, a Christmas party, a Halloween party, or a graduation party. But have you ever considered a reading party? It's easy and fun—and it's unique. Kids love it. It might even become an annual event at your home. Following are some ideas you might want to consider as you plan such a party.

Guests Encourage your children to invite classmates and cousins, neighbors and friends. Make your own invitations or fliers featuring pictures of familiar book covers or a computer-drawing of a book or books. State the date and time, location and purpose, and the name and phone number of the party-givers. Ask everyone to bring a book and to either read a favorite passage or page from the book or be prepared to tell in their own words what they like best about the book.

Location The party may be in a neighborhood park, backyard, family room or any other room in your home, or a rented facility. Decorate festively.

Program Feature a professional storyteller as part of the festivities or read or tell a story yourself—one that a wide range of children will be interested in. You might add puppets, a felt board, or dramatization to heighten the experience. This would be a great way for adolescents and teenagers to participate.

Activity   Give each child some paper and colored pencils, and have them draw a picture representing some aspect of the book they brought. Then ask them to share in pairs or small groups. Give each one who participates a small prize—such as a bookmark or a pencil and notebook for writing their own stories.

Refreshments   This will be as simple or as elaborate as you wish. Cookies and lemonade would be sufficient, or you could serve lunch outdoors or go to a neighborhood park for a picnic. If you prefer, each child might bring some food to share.

Record Keeper   As the guests leave, ask them to sign a guest book (that you or your children make ahead of time). Encourage them to add any comments they may wish. This record can be a permanent reminder of the event and even provide an incentive to hold another reading party the following year.

A Family Affair   Include even the youngest members of the family. Preschoolers can help serve food and pass out paper and markers, or napkins and cups. One could be in charge of the guest book. Include them in the reading or sharing process as well. Younger children often provide the spark that will ignite older children to participate fully.

Read to Children in Your Community

Your family may wish to volunteer to read to children or adults in literacy programs, schools, shelters, hospitals, or orphanages in your neighborhood or town. Call the office of your local newspaper, or ask your librarian for names and phone numbers of existing programs and agencies where your services would be welcome. Then call the organizations to find out what they need and how your family may contribute. Here are some to consider:

Hospitals Thousands of children are in hospitals and treatment centers around the country. Many are recovering from surgery or are part of a physical rehabilitation program or other form of treatment. They would welcome a storyteller or someone to read to them—especially other children. Find out what your children can do to bring a bit of sunshine to a child who is shut in. The experience will bless not only the recipients, but the givers as well.

Orphanages Several churches in southern California are involved with orphanages in Tijuana and Ensenada, Mexico. These children are starved for books and toys and new friends to interact with. If you are in a border city and can help orphans in Mexico or children in other shelters, look into the reading and friendship-building opportunities they present.

Native American Reservations   If you live in an area near a reservation, inquire about how they might use you as a reader or as a volunteer in reading programs in their schools. If you can share books about the Native American culture and traditions, all the better.

Juvenile Crisis Intervention Centers   In major cities around the country there are centers that specialize in rehabilitation and treatment for children and young adults recovering from substance abuse or in some other transition from a life crisis. You could make an enormous difference to these children by sharing books and friendship through reading.

Homeless Shelters   According to reports by the National Coalition for the Homeless, nearly eighty thousand homeless children do not attend school regularly. The majority of these children live in shelters for the homeless. Many do not have access to library books, and most probably do not have books of their own.

Your family could donate books you no longer need or want, or contribute money toward buying books for these children, or offer to read to them. You could organize a reading team or group from your church, school, community, or Scout troop and conduct a story hour once a week or each month, as time and resources are available. Many homeless children are as starved for companionship and cultural experiences as they are for a home of their own.

Project Open Book

If the children of homeless families are of special concern to you, you and your children may want to volunteer your time and services to them through an established network called Project Open Book, created by Reading Is Fundamental.

Launched in 1980 in response to the special educational needs of homeless children, this project set up "reading corners" in a variety of transitional and emergency shelters for the homeless. In the past fourteen years, the project has expanded to include a variety of sites where books are not readily available to children and their parents. These might include transitional houses, havens for battered women and their children, schools for the homeless, after-school programs, and public health clinics.

Book publishers and distributors donate thousands of books, magazines, and reference materials each year to Project Open Book. The materials are then distributed to Open Book sites throughout the United States.

Volunteers at each site set up a reading corner and an informal library for families and their children to use freely. They also provide books for individuals to keep. For children with few or no toys or other possessions, imagine what a treasure a new book would be!

Project Open Book also provides free bookmarks, posters, and brochures to encourage family reading. As a volunteer you could talk to parents and their children about the pleasure and importance of reading and how to enjoy it as an individual or with another family member.

For more information, write to:

Open Book
Reading Is Fundamental
1600 Maryland Avenue, SW
Suite 600
Washington, DC 20024

Discuss
the Theme
of a Book

Theme, according to late children's writer Lee Wyndham, is the "melody, the motive, the dominant *idea*" one develops through a story. Theme is what the story is about. And theme provides a wonderful avenue for conversation and communication. After reading a book with your children or talking with them about a book they have read, ask them what the book was about. Encourage them to look for the basic message or meaning of the story, and see if they can state it in a sentence or two.

Examples of familiar story themes include:

- Long-term friendship is better than short-term popularity.
- Understanding yourself leads to understanding others.
- Through wit and courage the weak can overcome the strong.

Stories that are most effective and memorable are those that meet these and other basic human needs. "Children's fundamental needs," said Wyndham, "are no different from yours and mine." They include such things as:

1. The Need to Love and Be Loved
   None of us ever outgrows this need. Whether or not it is

fulfilled, it forever affects our relationships and attitudes toward others.

2. The Need to Belong

Children everywhere need first to be accepted by their families and then by their peers. Feeling deprived of acceptance can lead children to all kinds of extreme behaviors.

3. The Need to Achieve

Each of us has a built-in desire to do or be something that will make a difference in life and result in a sense of personal worth and satisfaction.

4. The Need for Security—Material, Emotional, Spiritual

Everyone wants to be free from anxiety and fear, to be connected to others on an emotional level, and to have a sense of values and moral purpose that comes from a foundation grounded in relationship with family and friends and a loving God.

5. The Need to Know

People everywhere share this basic need to know the how and why of life around them. It is the reason for reading, for seeking education, for taking up hobbies, and for exploring the unknown, the unusual, and the unfamiliar.

Lead your children in a discussion of the story theme and encourage them to relate it to their own life and needs. You will help them gain insight into themselves and others, and you will also gain insight into their needs and perhaps find new and better ways to help meet them.

Discover
and Use
Reference Books

You don't have to be a walking encyclopedia for your children, though at times you may wish you were! Children are curious—as you know. They look for answers to everything from why a blade of grass stands up straight to why the stars stay in the sky.

You can help them research the answers to these and other curiosities by introducing them to reference books. They can learn to find out what they need to know quickly and easily from a variety of sources. For example, did you know the following books may be found on the reference shelves of most public libraries?

- *Facts about the Presidents*
- *Who's Who in America*
- *Children's Books in Print* (three volumes: subject, author, title)
- *Directory of Special Libraries*
- *Contemporary Authors*

To find just the right volume for the answers to the questions your children have, train them to do a bit of detective work on their own—to make a plan.

For example, suppose your ten-year-old son is curious about birds' feathers. He needs some fast facts to include in a report on how birds differ from other animals. Feathers happen to be the one distinguishing feature.

Encourage him to write down exactly what he needs for the report—a definition of the word *feather,* a description of different kinds of feathers, the feather count in various species, and any other fascinating or unfamiliar facts available. Some appropriate books on feathers may be in the reference section. Others may be on the regular shelves. Some reference books are more suitable for adult readers or specialists in a field. Others are for people who want basic information, not an in-depth study. A librarian can be helpful with this selection.

The point, however, is to show your children that the answer to almost any question they have on any topic can be located in printed form. They simply need to know what to ask and where to ask it.

Children can access information data bases by computer, as well, but I think it's important to show our children that even computerized data is generally compiled from a printed source. This is an opportunity to demonstrate the power and value of the written word.

You may also want to consider asking for reference discards for your family. Inquire at your library about its replacement policy. If you are willing to carry away some of the discarded volumes, a librarian might be happy to notify you when he or she is ready to replace them. Generally, a recent edition of any reference book still has enough useful information to be valuable to your children. The book itself is also a practical tool for showing them how to use reference books to gather information.

PART 3

Foster Reading Enrichment

Write a Family Narrative

Writing fosters reading just as reading motivates writing. Children who write are generally children who read. To encourage the link between the two, invite your children to participate, perhaps even lead the way, in writing a story or keeping a journal of your family's life. You can do this in different ways. Two that come to mind are:

1. Chronology Begin with the formation of the family unit: marriage of the parents, births of the children, changes in family structure that would be affected by a death or divorce or an adoption. Parents can enter their impressions and responses, and children may add to the narrative as they are able and desire to do so.

Or ask one family member to be the official recorder. That person assumes the responsibility for creating the narrative, keeping it going, and blending all the material into a cohesive unit. Individuals can participate by providing the recorder with details they want to see included.

You may want to create a box with a stack of paper nearby so family members can write down their responses, impressions, and memories to be included in the narrative.

2. Category Select topics that represent your family's interests. For example, you might have separate sections in a notebook marked: Vacations, Celebrations, Hobbies, Significant Events, Milestones, and so on. Each person can add to the entry as he or she wishes to. An adult or older teen could supervise the book and keep it up-to-date and available, perhaps even eliciting contributions from family members.

If you wish to embellish the narrative, add photos, captions, cartoon drawings, or pictures from magazines. Even very young children can participate. They can draw a picture, make a border for a page, add colorful stickers, or tell their feelings and impressions to an older person who can add to the narrative for them.

The purpose of starting and maintaining a family narrative is to give parents and children the opportunity to document their life together—to enrich their sense of heritage and community and to express their individuality.

More Family Writing Activities

Holiday Letters If you enjoy sending a letter to friends and family during the holiday season or at some other time, include your children in the process. Perhaps each one can add a paragraph and photo or sketch, recounting the highlights of his or her year. You can edit the final copy.

Pen Pals My mother, who lived in the United States as a child, corresponded through the years with a cousin of about her age who lived in Ireland. The two exchanged letters for more than fifty years. Then during their sixties they had the joy of meeting in person when my mother visited Ireland. A special bond, different from other forms of communication, is formed by writing letters. Encourage your children to find a pen pal—perhaps a relative or friend in another state or country—to write to. It can be an enriching experience for both.

Travel Journal Maintain a family journal while traveling. Let everyone contribute what they see and feel. Children may want to add a sketch as well. This is a wonderful souvenir that the entire family will enjoy looking at, reading, and going back to time and again.

Family Notes and News   Encourage your children to write notes to one another. You take the lead. Write to your sons and daughters when they are away at camp or visiting a grandparent or friend. Stick a love note in their shoe or lunch box. Write a poem or letter to your children on their birthdays. Be sure to date each one, and encourage them to save them in a book. What a heritage this will be later in life. You may wish to accompany each letter with a current photo of the child or the entire family.

Letter Writing   Today it is so easy to pick up the phone and call someone, to communicate over modem, or to send a fax, that the art of old-fashioned letter writing seems nearly lost. But you can introduce your children to this wonderful pastime by providing the supplies and space they need to experiment with it. You may even wish to take out a book on letter writing from the library or ask the librarian for a book of published letters.

Provide a work space, including a desk or simple table and chairs. Stock it with paper, pencils, pens, colored markers, erasers, envelopes, and stamps. Fill a box with writing paper and note cards of various sizes. If you wish to add a creative touch, put out some stickers, crayons, colored pencils, and stamp pads. Be sure to set out a wastepaper basket as well.

If you have a computer or typewriter available, your children may want to type and print out their letters. This will appeal to many boys and girls who see handwriting as drudgery. And since computers allow them to edit and replace words and phrases easily, they may participate with greater enthusiasm.

Write a Book Review

Children who read have opinions about what they read. Encourage them to write down their thoughts and ideas as they finish a book. This does not have to be a tedious process, but, rather, it can be an experience that extends and enriches their reading process. You can file the reviews for others to refer to, read them aloud during a family time, or post them on a bulletin board in the reading corner.

Here are some ideas to stimulate your children to think about and respond to the books they read. You can adjust the questions for different ages, temperaments, or individual needs.

1. Title, author, publisher, type of book (i.e., mystery, science information, adventure, sports biography)
2. Why did you choose this book?
3. Describe the point or theme of this book in one sentence.
4. How would you rate this book for entertainment?
   Low High
   1 2 3 4 5 (Circle the number that best fits.)
5. How would you rate this book for information?
   Low High
   1 2 3 4 5 (Circle the number that best fits.)
6. What do you know about the author after reading this book?

7. Would you recommend this book to another person? Why?
8. Did you learn anything new about yourself or about life from this book? If so, what did you learn?
9. Would you read another book of this kind?
10. Would you read another book by this author?

When someone has read a book, whether it be a delight or a dud, he or she is usually eager to talk about it. Book reviews are just one more way to foster reading enrichment in your family and to hook your kids on books.

Keep
a Diary of
Books Read

An adult friend of mine is a movie buff. He is proud to tell anyone who inquires (and many who don't!) that he views one thousand movies a year—roughly three a day. He is retired now, and aside from hiking and walking, movies are his passion. To keep track of the movies he has watched over the past ten years, he records the title of each one in a notebook, the date he watched it, a sentence or two about the plot, and his impressions.

"That way," he says, "I can check my list before choosing a movie. I know at a glance whether or not I've seen it and if so, how I felt about it. Sometimes I watch a movie twice—but it has to be pretty good for me to do that—because there are still so many I haven't seen." Now there's a man dedicated to his pastime. It's no longer a hobby—it's serious business!

After listening to him talk, I realized that his method of tracking his interest is a sound one. Any reader could benefit from the same kind of documentation. The written word is an excellent way to record and remember important experiences and events in our lives.

Encourage your children to do something similar with the books they read. What a wealth of information and impressions they will collect throughout their childhood—or if they continue, over a lifetime. I wish I had done this when I was growing up.

In high school my English instructor asked us to write down five books we had read in the past five years—and to add a few details about the books themselves and why they were significant. At the time I was not an avid reader, and at first I couldn't think of more than two titles. If I had had a book log, however, it would have been easy to answer that question in detail.

Your children might also enjoy making a daily entry in a "book diary" established exclusively to record their thoughts and impressions about the books they are reading—as they read.

Whatever method they adopt, be supportive. They may wish to share their entries with you, or ask you to read a particular book so you can talk about it with them. Writing, conversing, and creating a written journal or log are just some of the ways you can continue to foster reading enrichment in your children's lives.

Apply Ideas Gained from Books

Children love to interact with their environment. They don't want simply to read about bugs; they want to touch them and watch them in motion. They want to climb the mountain they read about. They want to bake the cookies they see on the pages of a book. Interaction is one of the major attractions to video games and write-your-own-ending books. Young people want to participate.

You can encourage this desire by getting involved with them. For example, when my oldest daughter was going through the Little House books by Laura Ingalls Wilder, she and I read many of them together. One Christmas we made the gingerbread recipe from one of Mrs. Wilder's books.

When my granddaughter Johannah turned four she and her mother planned a party from *The Tea Party Book*. The book is filled with unusual and entertaining party ideas for little children. Among Johannah's favorites were the royal tea party and the teddy bear tea party. So they combined the two and held a royal teddy bear tea party. They made the foods, invitations, and decorations and asked each guest to dress up like a king or queen and to bring along a favorite stuffed bear. For favors they handed out paper crowns and scepters. It was a great success, especially for Johannah, who ate everything on her plate including the delicate cucumber and cream cheese finger sandwiches that the other preschoolers passed up. (They didn't *say* they were gross, but the expressions on their faces left no doubt.) Imagine the warm and delightful memories Johannah will have for the rest of her life. Her mother didn't simply read her a book about parties. The book became the incentive and the vehicle for a party of her very own.

When my son, Jim, was about ten or twelve he became interested in magic tricks. I remember the many hours he spent at the magic store and the library in search of books on how to perfect his performance. That led to a small neighborhood business. He invited children to our backyard where he wielded his magic wand, waved his top hat, and produced long strings of colored scarves and nickels and dimes and playing cards out of nowhere. My mother even made him a cape for his birthday with the words "Houdini Sweeney" (Sweeney is his last name) embroidered on the back. I believe he still has it in his box of childhood treasures.

Think of the creative things you and your children can do. Your interaction may take the form of a vacation, a craft such as paper folding or knitting or sewing; food preparation, including cooking and baking; hobbies, such as stamp collecting; assembling a scrapbook on a favorite topic; putting together a model airplane, train, or car; or playing a game or sport.

Do a Book-Related Art Project

Through the years of my writing career I have visited many elementary schools to speak to students about my life as an author. I remember one visit in particular because the teacher and the children expressed an unusual amount of creativity and hospitality on my behalf.

As I entered the multi-purpose room for my talk, I noticed a number of tables set with place mats made out of the covers of my books. The students had made copies of the covers and laminated each one, creating a washable surface, ideal for a place mat. Following my talk, we enjoyed a light dessert and they presented me with a place mat for myself and one for each member of my family.

That is just one way to extend the reading experience. You might also consider some of the following:

- Make a shadow box, depicting a scene from a favorite story.
- Create a paper bag puppet of a character from a book.
- Make a collage of words and pictures that characterize a book.
- Paint a wall mural.
- Do a finger painting of a scene from a book.
- Make paper costumes depicting some story characters.

- Make a bookmark out of colored construction paper glued to lightweight cardboard. Decorate it with a drawing or felt pieces or colored yarn made into the shape of a character or animal from a book.
- Make clay figures of characters in a book.

Extend the experience to your neighborhood, school, youth group, Sunday school class, or Scout troop. Invite other children over for a story hour. Have them each bring a story they wish to share through art. Show them how to make one or more of the crafts listed. Directions for these and similar activities can be found in any simple craft book or children's encyclopedia. Guests could work individually or in pairs or groups and then present their story and accompanying artwork to the rest of the children.

Decorate with Book Mobiles

Help your children draw pictures or create small items from a favorite story or book to be used in a homemade mobile. For example, after reading a book about insects, they could make paper insects that resemble the creatures they read about. For fiction they might draw a picture of a character or a prop that character is known for; for example, Linus and his blanket in the Charlie Brown books, Madeline's coat from the Madeline series, the cat from *The Cat in the Hat,* and so on. Here are some easy mobiles to create and assemble.

Animal Book Mobile Choose four animals that your child can identify from books you have on hand or have borrowed from the library. Cut out pictures of these animals from a coloring book or magazine, or the child may make her own drawings. Color the picture, back it with cardboard, and hang with string from a coat hanger.

Book Cover Mobile Purchase paperback children's books from a thrift or resale book shop, garage sale, or a library fund-raiser. You can sometimes pick up individual titles for as little as a quarter or fifty cents each. Take off the covers of the books. Fasten each one to a length of lightweight string and stretch across the room or around the book corner for a decorative effect. This is something you can change often because it is so inexpensive to make.

Paper Chain Mobile Draw pictures of characters and scenes from favorite stories. Then cut pictures in 1½-inch strips. Link together and fasten ends with glue to form a paper chain. Hang from the ceiling in different lengths, or use it to frame a bedroom window.

Encourage Your Child to Write a Book

 I am grateful to my third-grade teacher for motivating me to write. I felt the first spark of desire to one day become a published writer the day she assigned us to write a book of our own and to illustrate it with our own drawings. I don't remember the title of my book, but I do remember the feeling it provoked. I ran home that day and shouted to my mother at the top of my lungs that I had written a pretend book, and I proudly showed it to her. "But someday," I said, "I want to write a real book that people can take out of the library and read."

Years later, after that dream had come true in my life, I led a writing workshop for second and third graders at a school in Oceanside, California. I explained to them the steps of the writing process—from idea to published book—that I had taken with two of my picture books, *Let's Take a Walk on the Beach* and *Let's Take a Walk in the City.* Here are those simple steps to use with your children.

1. Think of an idea you wish to write about by looking at your experience and those things you are interested in or know something about. For example, I lived near the city as a child. As an adult I now live near the beach. These are two places that have special memories for me, so I wanted to write about a child who spends a day at the beach and one who

spends a day in the city, and how each one learns about his five senses through the experience of walking through the city or walking along the beach.

2. Think of a couple of characters to put into your story. I thought about my nephew, Lanty, and his mother. I knew what Lanty liked, what he was curious about, and what things he might like to experience if he were in the city or at the beach for a day with his mother.

3. Think of some dialogue for the characters so they will talk during the story. I could imagine what Lanty and his mom would say if they were shopping in the city or swimming at the beach.

4. Think of some actions for the characters so they will not be stuck in one place. I moved the characters from one setting to another as they walked down the city street and strolled along the beach. In the city book, the boy and his mother looked at the toys in the store window, listened to the city traffic noises, smelled the aroma of fresh-baked goods in the bakery, ate pizza for lunch, and touched the soft mittens and furry lining of the boots they bought.

5. Think of an ending that will show the characters finishing what they started and feeling satisfied.

The students wanted to write their own version of *Let's Take a Walk* . . . so we decided on a title together—*Let's Take a Walk in the Mall*. Teachers agreed that the children would work on this idea in the classroom, following my suggestions. I was delighted, and the kids were thrilled at the possibility of becoming authors themselves.

About two weeks later I received a package in the mail from the students' teacher. The manila envelope was stuffed with little books, *Let's Take a Walk in the Mall*, written by the children in her class. They had followed the simple process and produced wonderful books, complete with their own drawings and text.

This exercise is especially well-suited to boys and girls between the ages of seven and ten. Encourage your children or students to do something similar—either write their own original story or a spin-off of a story they have read and enjoyed.

Create
a Skit
Based
on a Book

When I was a child, my sister and I and our two close friends put on a neighborhood play each summer for years. Our audience had to use their imagination as much as we did. We had no props, a few dress-up clothes from our mothers' discards, some fabric swatches, and a couple of old blankets to designate the setting. The red blanket was a house, as I recall, and the green one was the school, and so on. We even sold tickets for ten cents each to cover the cost of the cookies and lemonade we served at intermission. Each summer the backyard of our Illinois home became the neighborhood theater.

I don't recall going off to buy or borrow a book of plays. We made up our own—ideas we generated from our experiences and interests, and from stories we read in books. Most of the time we did our own version of a familiar story, but the incentive came from what we read. Books played an important part of our ability to imagine and dream and create.

Years later when I was a young mother, my own children delighted in playing dress-up, parading around the house and yard with cast-off clothing, too-big shoes, and sparkling necklaces and gaudy earrings from the bottom of my jewelry box.

They, too, loved to act out a story or a familiar play. I remember one night when the whole family got involved. The children were the lead characters, and my husband and I were bit players.

Now, more than two decades later, our grandchildren love to play dress-up and to act out stories and plays. Not long ago when I was baby-sitting we read *Peter Pan* and *The Little Mermaid*. After we finished reading we acted out the stories. What fun it was for me to be a child again and to participate in their playacting. I was reminded of the importance of encouraging our children's imagination.

What better way than to blend reading and pretending? Children can even create a skit based on an information book. Suppose they enjoy reading about sharks or whales or plants or cars or history or a famous person. Talk to them about what they have read and ask them to *show* rather than tell the information. Encourage your children to demonstrate how a shark or whale moves and how they use their mouths to capture food. Ask your child to create a skit or to do a pantomime of a favorite character (real or imaginary) from a book, or to recreate a scene from the life of a person they have read about.

If we want to get our kids hooked on books, we need to start now while they are young and eager and imaginative—and teachable. Creating skits is an excellent way to appeal to young people of all ages.

Rewrite the Ending of a Book

Some current and popular books of fiction for children stop before the end—on purpose. They are written to stimulate young people to use their imagination to create the ending, based on what they have read so far. Other books provide readers with a choice of endings. Some computer programs offer this option as well. Still other books provide an opportunity to interact with the plot along the way. They offer the reader options as she or he reads.

This device seems to be especially effective for reluctant readers. If other techniques fail to motivate your child, consider the open-ended story. It is also a useful method for stimulating imagination and creative writing.

But you don't need a book with a device to encourage your children to use their imagination. They can simply rewrite the ending of an existing book. Consider some of these well-known stories and the potential consequences for the characters if the story ended differently. Discuss the possibilities with your children when they finish reading. These sample questions can stimulate a lively discussion about possible alternatives. Young people can start with these well-known plots or use them to stimulate the process of creating a new ending for a story they are currently reading.

- *Charlotte's Web* by E. B. White

How would this story have been different if Charlotte hadn't died?

- *The Diary of Anne Frank* by Anne Frank
  What might have happened had Anne escaped capture by the Nazis?
- *Ramona, the Pest* by Beverly Cleary
  How would the Quimby household have been different if Ramona had not caused so much mischief?
- *Daniel Boone* by James Daugherty
  What might have happened to Daniel if he had not learned so well the habits of the Native Americans who lived nearby?
- *Treasure Island* by Robert Louis Stevenson
  What might have happened to Jim Hawkins if he had not been able to stand up to Long John Silver?

Question and answer sessions stimulate imagination and critical thinking skills, which children will use throughout their lifetime.

Create a Book-Centered Birthday Party

Enrich your children's appreciation of reading by organizing a birthday party around books. This party idea is probably most suitable for children aged seven to eleven. Following are suggestions for the reading theme.

1. Compile a list of age-appropriate books by consulting with the librarian at your public school or at the local branch library.
2. Use the books as decorations. Stand them up on tables around the party room. Or make copies of the book covers and mount them on posts, walls, furniture, or over doorways.
3. Hire a storyteller or give yourself or an older teen that job. Choose a book or story that is appropriate for the ages of the guests. You probably will not have time to read an entire book at such a time (unless it's a picture book), but you may read portions of it or a story from a magazine.
4. Play a reading-related game. Gather everyone in a circle. In the center place a box or basket with various kinds of children's books, each one in a plain paper bag:
   - a sport book
   - a book about cars or trucks
   - a fantasy
   - a book about dinosaurs

- a mystery story
- a science fiction book
- an animal book
- a book about a city or foreign country

Start with the birthday child. Ask her to choose a bag with a book and then to step out of the room to look at the book and formulate three clues to the topic of the book. When the child returns, she gives the first clue. The others guess. If no one gets the right answer, she gives clue number 2 and so on. If no one guesses correctly, the birthday child gets five points.

If someone does guess correctly, the guesser gets five points. Keep score because the child with the most correct answers wins a prize at the end—a paperback book of his or her choice. Continue around the circle, giving each person a chance to participate.

Example: The birthday child may draw a book about dinosaurs. Her clues could be something like these, each one providing progressively more information:

A. The subject of a scary movie.
B. A powerful creature.
C. An animal that lived on earth a long time ago.

By that time someone probably would have guessed dinosaurs. But if not, the birthday child gets five points and it's the next person's turn.

5. Serve refreshments that carry out the reading theme. You could make or buy a cake decorated like a book cover, or serve cupcakes with a book decoration of some kind on top.
6. Give out party favors such as bookmarks, book posters, or used paperback books purchased at a garage sale or at a used book store.

Write a Character Profile

Another way to enrich your children's reading experiences is to encourage them to create a profile of one of their favorite characters from a story, the Bible, or a book they have enjoyed. They can extend the activity by writing a profile of two opposing characters to see the contrast in motives, appearances, actions, beliefs, moods, and so on.

Here are some guidelines you can use or adapt to suit the project. I will use one of the characters in a recent book of mine as an example.

1. **Book title and author:** The Green Team by Karen O'Connor
2. **Name and age of the chosen character:** Mitch, eight years old
3. **Outstanding physical characteristics:** Dark brown hair, blue eyes, slim build, a bit tall for his age
4. **Outstanding behavioral characteristics:** Quick thinking, fast talking, on the move, in and out of trouble throughout the story, impatient with his sister, Molly, wants to do what is right, willing to make amends when he does something wrong, fun to be around because he is always ready for action.

5. Most appealing traits: Mitch is creative and curious. He seems like someone kids would like to be friends with.

Your child can stop there or go further. Older students, usually ten and up, might want to go into more depth. They can add the following:

6. Clothing:
7. Voice and speech patterns:
8. Hobbies and interests:
9. Kinds of friends:
10. Favorite movies and books:

Some of the details listed may not be found in the story, but your children can use their imagination here, gleaning greater insight into the character through what is known in the story. This exercise will increase their insight and awareness and their ability to discern the strengths and weaknesses of people in their life as well.

Write a Letter to a Favorite Author

 Many children's writers receive wonderful letters from their readers. Fan mail is one of the highlights of their professional lives. Since most writers work in isolation, letters from readers are especially welcome.

Perhaps your children would enjoy writing a letter to one of their favorite authors. They can write to him or her in care of the company that publishes the author's books. To locate the address of the publishing house, check the listing in *Writer's Market*.

You can help your children write the letter if they are too young, or simply be on hand to support older ones if they need help.

It is natural for a parent to correct grammar or punctuate sentences or even want to rewrite some of the paragraphs. But if you can hold back, do so. It is important to let the children write from their hearts and to express themselves as authentically as they can. If they ask for spelling or punctuation help, give it. But if they don't, let their letters stand as written.

The purpose of the letter is not to present a perfect piece of writing but to encourage and validate their interest in literature and reading. Being in contact with a real live author can be a very special part of the overall experience—made richer if they receive a response.

Here are a few excerpts from letters I've received over the years. They've warmed my heart and encouraged me on days when I thought I'd run out of ideas and energy.

Dear Ms. O'Connor,

Thank you for your book about Sally Ride. She's a neat lady. I like the part when she went down the tube into the water with sharks. Do all astronauts have to do that? If they do then I don't want to be one anymore.

Maria

Dear Ms. O'Connor,

I never read a nonfiction book until I met you. I like stories instead. But you made it seem like fun to read nonfiction. I'm going to take a nonfiction book out of our library. It's my first one ever.

John

Dear Ms. O'Connor,

Thank you for talking to our class about being an author. Are you famous, like the president of the United States? Do you have a bodyguard when you go grocery shopping? Please write me back and answer these questions.

Louis

As you can see, the more spontaneous and authentic letters are to the children's experience and emotions, the more precious those letters are to the author.

Read to the Elderly

Many older people would enjoy being read to. Some can't read to themselves anymore because of failing eyesight or an inability to hold a book. Others would simply like the companionship that a shared reading experience creates. You may have access to the elderly in your family, or through church and community groups, or you might contact directors of senior clubs and retirement and elder-care facilities in your city.

In San Diego one of the local CBS television news affiliates sponsors a community outreach program called 10 Friends. It brings together children and the elderly—for conversation, art projects, activities, reading. Both age groups enjoy the attention and friendship that results from sharing time together.

A program of this type could be started in any community. It can be large enough to include several student and senior groups or very simple and focused. Perhaps you could unite a Scout troop or youth group with men and women from a facility for the elderly.

If you prefer something smaller yet, you and your children could simply volunteer to read to the elderly in small groups or in partnerships one afternoon or evening a month. Or children can put on a poetry reading—sharing some of their own writing as well as poems of published writers. They might combine the reading with an accompanying skit or short play.

The purpose is to provide children with another opportunity to enrich their reading experiences and to share them with other people. If your children are interested in this idea, let them be part of the process. Together you can locate facilities that might be interested. Look in the Yellow Pages of your local phone book, or use a city resource guide, usually available at the library. Send a letter to the director explaining your idea and including a flier detailing what you would like to do. A few days later, follow up with a phone call.

Here are some items to include in your plan.

- Time and available dates, e.g., the first Monday of the month from 4:00 to 5:00 P.M.
- Schedule of readings:
  January 3   Poetry
  February 7   A mystery story
  March 7   A children's picture book
- Time of fellowship and refreshments (we'll provide!)

This will give the activity director a concrete proposal to consider and share with the residents. Include your name, address, and phone number, and let the director know you'll be calling in a few days to talk it over.

This is a chance to reach out to the elderly, to express care, to enrich their mental and emotional lives, and to give your children an opportunity to stretch and grow as well.

Organize a Used Book Drive and Donate the Books

Help your children look for ways to put books into the hands of others—especially those less fortunate than they. A used book drive is a great way to do this.

In your neighborhood alone many families probably have books they no longer want or need or have space for. You and your children could pass the word that you are organizing a book drive and will donate all books received to organizations such as:

- a children's hospital
- an orphanage
- a school
- needy families
- a homeless shelter
- reputable organizations such as the YMCA, Salvation Army, or Goodwill

Choose a drop-off site (maybe your garage, if suitable), or offer to pick up books during certain hours and on specified dates.

Once the books are in, sort them (baby books, children's, young adults, adults), and box or bag them accordingly. Then call the agency or group you wish to donate to and make arrangements for delivery. Get your kids involved from start to finish. Participation will heighten their awareness and motivate them to share the joy and self-confidence that reading and learning generate.

Options to Consider

1. Round up used books from neighbors and friends, sell them to a used book dealer, and donate the profits (and leftover books) to one of the above groups or a charity of your choice.
2. Have a used book sale in your backyard. Invite neighbors, family, and friends. Use the profits to buy new books for a needy family or as a gift for your school or church library.
3. Ask local authors to donate an autographed copy of one of their books to your book drive. Hold a book auction for neighbors and friends. Donate proceeds to a charity.
4. Contact local authors, as above, but instead of auctioning their books, donate them to a charity or library at a homeless shelter or orphanage or inner-city school.

Organize a Reading-Related Holiday Gift Fair

Round up your children, and those in your neighborhood, and help them earn money for holiday spending. Attract customers with a colorful banner on your garage or window or fliers in mailboxes—or both.

SEE US FIRST!
BOOKS 'N' STUFF
from the Johnson kids
Great prices! Great gifts!
Shop early for the best selection
of used books and handmade gifts.
Saturday. 9:00 to 12:00
Johnsons' backyard

1. Provide a selection of used books that you may have on hand or purchase at a used bookstore and resell for a small profit.
2. Make decorative bookmarks out of felt scraps or heavy construction paper or poster board. Charge twenty-five to fifty cents apiece, depending on materials and time involved.
3. Sell coupon books. The person who purchases the book makes good on each coupon. These could include the following: "good for one bedtime story"; "good for one book of your choice at Tom's Bookstore—value $10.00"; "good for a visit to the art museum during the children's book illustrator's art show"; or "good for one evening at the children's puppet

show at the library." Find out what reading-related programs are available in your community library and at bookstores and schools, and create a few coupons that will include those options.

Eight to ten coupons per book seems about right. You can have more than one of a kind in each book, since some choices will be more popular than others. Decorate the coupon book cover, bind it with staples, and charge $2.00—or whatever seems fair—for each booklet.

Start a Neighborhood Children's Book Club

Every reader can benefit from outside support. Young readers especially need it as the world of media and technology vies for their attention. To foster this support in your family and neighborhood, consider organizing a neighborhood book club for children.

The structure of the group can be as formal or as informal as you wish. Start by inviting neighborhood kids and their parents to a picnic in your yard or at a nearby park. Each one can bring his or her own lunch, or you and your children can provide the meal. Limit participation to the boys and girls you know well, or open it to anyone in the area who is interested. It's probably best to start small and see what response you get, then enlarge it as you feel more secure and inquiries come in.

Decide on a time and place to meet (the same location each week or month, or rotate homes or yards among the members). The agenda can be very simple: a few minutes to get acquainted and to welcome any newcomers, announcement of the topic of the day (mysteries, sports, science, nature, and so on), showing of other books related to this topic or genre in order to stimulate members to expand their knowledge, the reading itself, sharing of personal impressions of the reading, closing comments, and refreshments.

Ways to Expand the Project

1. Create a buddy system. Encourage book club members to read together between meetings and share some of the books they enjoy.
2. Spread the word and invite new members. Welcome newcomers with a flier that details how the club works and what is expected of them.
3. Have a make-and-do day, creating crafts or preparing food based on material found in the books read.
4. Encourage show-and-share. Every few weeks or months, or whenever you feel motivated, ask members to bring in a favorite book and to talk about it for a minute or two in front of the group.

Whatever you choose to do from the selections presented in this book, you are sure to enrich the life of every child you touch, and to enrich your own life as well. I hope you enjoy the process.

About the Author

Karen O'Connor is an award-winning author of over thirty books for children and adults. She has been involved with young people as a mother, teacher, youth leader, and tutor, as well. Currently, Karen lives in San Diego, California, where she and her husband enjoy walking along the beach, hiking in the mountains, and playing with their nine grandchildren.